THRESHOLDS

UMBRALES

poems by
Claribel Alegría

translation by Darwin Flakoll

CURBSTONE PRESS

FIRST EDITION, 1996
translation copyright © 1996 by Claribel Alegría
All Rights Reserved

Printed in Canada on acid-free paper by Best Book Manufacturers
Cover design and illustration: Stephanie Church

Curbstone Press is a 501(c)(3) nonprofit publishing house
whose programs are supported in part by private donations and
by grants from: ADCO Foundation, Witter Bynner Foundation
for Poetry, Connecticut Commission on the Arts, Connecticut
Arts Endowment Fund, The Ford Foundation, The Greater
Hartford Arts Council, Junior League of Hartford, Lawson
Valentine Foundation, LEF Foundation, Lila Wallace-Reader's
Digest Literary Publishers Marketing Development Program
administered by CLMP, The Andrew W. Mellon Foundation,
National Endowment for the Arts, Puffin Foundation, and
United Way-Windham Region.

Library of Congress Cataloging-in-Publication Data

Alegría, Claribel.
    [Unbrales. English & Spanish]
    Umbrales = Thresholds : poems / by Claribel Alegría ; translation
by Darwin J. Flakoll.—1st ed.
        p.   cm.
    Poems in English and Spanish on alternate pages.
    ISBN 1-880684-36-5 (alk. paper)
    I. Flakoll, D. J. (Darwin J.) II. Title.
PQ7539.A47A24   1997
861—dc20   96-21329

published by
CURBSTONE PRESS   321 Jackson Street   Willimantic, CT 06226
phone: (860) 423-5110   e-mail: curbston@connix.com
WWW at http://www.connix.com/~curbston/

THRESHOLDS / UMBRALES

A Bud, mi guía, mi amor,
mi todo

To Bud, my love,
my everything

*Sal de tu tierra y de tu
parentela y de la casa de tu
padre y ven a la tierra que te
mostraré.*

*"Go from your country and your
kindred and your father's
house to the land that I will
show you."*
GENESIS 12:1

"Follow your bliss."
Joseph Campbell

THRESHOLDS

UMBRALES

I · LA CEIBA

¿Cómo olvidar esa mañana
en que asaltaron mi pecho
las mariposas?
Una se posó en mi mano
habría podido cerrar los dedos
sobre ella
y atraparla
pero voló
voló.

Años atrás
avanzando insegura
sobre las baldosas chocolate
Rilke vibrando entre mis manos
floreciendo el hibisco
y el jazmín
detrás de la araucaria
una luna fantasma
recortada en pedazos
por las ramas
creí haber atrapado
la poesía
pero voló
voló.

Fue en Glasgow
sólo a mí me asaltaron
las mariposas locas
los niños me miraban

I · THE CEIBA

How forget that morning
when butterflies swarmed over my breast?
One lit on my hand
I could have closed my fingers
and trapped her
but she flew
she flew.

Years earlier
advancing hesitantly
over the chocolate tiles
Rilke vibrating in my hands
the hibiscus and jasmine
flowering
a phantasmal moon
behind the araucaria
sliced in pieces
by its branches
I believed I had entrapped poetry
but it flew
it flew.

It was in Glasgow
the crazed butterflies
only attacked me
children stared

con ojos dilatados.
¿Por qué? me pregunté
sintiéndome aturdida
¿por qué a mí me eligieron?
Es la blusa
lo supe
mi blusa con hojas otoñales.
¿Pero el milagro?
¿Quién me explica el milagro?
¿Por qué la mariposa
se posó en mi mano?

Después de aquella noche
en el patio sombrío de la casa
con la luna mirándome
a través de la araucaria
empecé a conjurar
palabras
a inventar mariposas
más nítidas unas que las otras
ninguna se amoldaba
a ese trazo interior
que vibra en mí.

Dejé la casa
dejé a los míos
a mis tibios aromas
a mis muertos.
Antes de mi partida

wide-eyed.
Why? I asked myself
in bewilderment
why did they choose me?
It was the blouse
I knew
my blouse with autumn leaves.
But the miracle?
Who can explain the miracle?
Why did the butterfly
alight on my hand?

After that night
in the darkened patio of the house
with the moon watching me
through the araucaria
I began to conjure up words
began to invent butterflies
some sharper than others
but none corresponded
to the vision
vibrating in me.

I left my home
left my people
my warm aromas
my dead.
Before my departure

mi padre
con los ojos nublados
me susurro al oído:
"no volverás"
me dijo
y me entregó un estuche
forrado en terciopelo
con una pluma fuente
entre el satén.
"Es tu espada
princesa".
¿Dijo princesa?
No
eso yo lo inventé
debiera haberlo dicho
porque en ese momento
me sentí Deirdre
de las desdichas.
"Es tu espada"
me dijo.

Sin darme mucha cuenta
tomé el destino entre mis manos
el tiempo no importaba
no importaba el espacio
el sabor de las palabras
importaba
mi pluma fuente-espada.

my father
with clouded eyes
whispered in my ear:
"You won't return,"
he said
and gave me
a velvet-lined case
with a fountain pen
nestling in the satin.
"This is your sword,
princess."
Did he say princess?
No
I invented it
but he should have said it
because at that moment
I felt I was Deirdre
of the Sorrows.
"This is your sword,"
he told me.

Almost without noticing
I took destiny in my hands
time didn't matter
nor did space
the flavor of words mattered
my fountain pen-sword.

Dejé la casa
antes de abandonarla
me detuve ante todos los espejos
era extraña mi imagen
desigual
como si se hubiesen encogido
los espejos,
como si estuviesen recelosos.
Salí en silencio
sin olvidar mi Rilke.
Me detuve un largo rato
ante la Ceiba
ante mi Ceiba protectora
que me sirvió de escudo
contra el sol
mientras con otros niños
y perros callejeros
y vendedoras ambulantes
nos congregábamos bajo sus ramas.
No había desconcierto
como en los laberintos del mercado
podíamos ser nosotros mismos
la Ceiba nos cubría
nos encubría
nos juntaba.
Su techo era el mapa
de mi patria
como ver dibujado en el aire

I left home
on the last day
I paused before all the mirrors
my image was strange
irregular
as if the mirrors had shrunk,
as if they distrusted me.
I left silently
without forgetting my Rilke.
I paused a long time
before the Ceiba
before my protective Ceiba
who shielded me
against the sun
while with other children
and stray dogs
and ambulant sales ladies
we gathered beneath its branches.
There was no chaos
as in the labyrinths
of the market place
we could be ourselves
the Ceiba covered us
sheltered us
brought us together.
Its roof was the map
of my homeland
like seeing sketched in the air

el mapa de mi patria
volandera.
Le prometí volver
refrescarme a su sombra
cuantas veces pudiera.
La Ceiba estaba quieta
ni una de sus hojas
se movió
pero sentí su bendición.
Desde su arboridad
me bendijo la Ceiba.

the restless map of my country.
I promised to return
to refresh myself in its shade
as often as I could.
The Ceiba was quiet
not a single leaf
stirred
but I felt its benediction.
From its treeness
the Ceiba blessed me.

II · EL RIO

Vino después el Río
el Río
y sus rumores
y su prisa
y sus barcos que vienen
y que van.
Eran anchas las riberas
de ese Río
y sé que es otro umbral
que hay que cruzar.
¿Cómo podré lograrlo?
Tuve miedo
y no tuve.
Yo sola frente al Río.
Me era extraño el paisaje
la lengua me era extraña
empecé a caminar por la ciudad
nadie me conocía
ni las calles
ni las casas
ni los rostros.
¿Hacia dónde iba?
¿Seguía siendo yo?
¿Estaba dando a luz
a esa otra yo
que fui después?
El Río frente a mí
era el mismo
y no era.

II · THE RIVER

Next came the River
the River
with its murmuring
its urgency
its ships coming
and going.
The margins of the River
were wide
and I knew it was another threshold
I had to cross.
How could I do it?
I was frightened
and yet I was not.
Alone facing the River.
The landscape was strange
the language foreign
I began walking through the city
nobody knew me
neither the streets
nor the houses
nor the faces.
Where was I going?
Was I still myself?
Was I giving birth
to that other self
I became?
The river before me
was the same
yet it wasn't.

Era río
era reto.

Con un pañuelo
anudado a la barbilla
se me acercó la vieja
desdentada
tenía surcos en el rostro
en la mirada.
"Soy pordiosera de milagros"
dijo acariciándome el cabello
"¿podrías darme uno"?
"Tuve un sueño hace rato,
soñé que me asaltaban las mariposas.
Una se posó en mi mano".
"Gracias"
dijo la vieja
me regaló una rosa
y con paso ligero
se esfumó.

It was river
it was challenge.

A toothless old lady
With a kerchief
knotted beneath her chin
approached me
there were furrows in her face
in her gaze.
"I am a beggar of miracles,"
she said stroking my hair
"can you give me one?"
"I had a dream a while ago,"
"I dreamt I was attacked by butterflies.
One lit in my hand."
"Thank you,"
the old lady said
she gave me a rose
and with rapid steps
she disappeared.

III · ABEJA-REINA

Navegué Río arriba
contra corriente
navegué
salté del barco
y empecé a caminar
por senderos peligrosos
me llevaba mi cuerpo
me arrastraba
no es que me hubiera fugado
de Santa Ana
de la Ceiba
del Río
simplemente mi cuerpo
me arrastraba.
Una noche
envuelta en una capa
y con sandalias
soñé que caminaba
por la arena
la arena era caliente
me quemaba los pies
y subí a un peñasco
y ví la luna
y brillaba mi piel
como la luna
y la luz de la luna
me quemaba.

III · QUEEN BEE

I sailed upstream
against the current
I sailed
jumped ashore
and began to wander
along perilous paths
my body impelled me
pulled me along
it wasn't that I had fled
from Santa Ana
from the Ceiba
from the River
it was simply my body
dragging me with it.
One night
clad in cape
and sandals
I dreamt I was walking
through the sand
the sand was hot
and scorched my feet
and I scaled a crag
and saw the moon
and my skin shone
like the moon
and the moonlight
burnt into me.

Me sentí abeja-reina al despertar:
zumbaba
corcoveaba.
Empecé a volar alto
descendía
me sentía asediada
por los zánganos
y volaba más alto
me convertía en llama
vacilaba
era el lenguaje escrito hace milenios
el lenguaje del cuerpo
enamorado
el vértigo
el dolor
el gozo hiriente
lloré con mis heridas
sentí la mordedura
de la trampa
el golpe de la piedra
lanzada a la deriva
pero también bailé
con la locura
con el espectro alado
de la muerte.
Los cinco sentidos me quemaban
el olor a albahaca era tan fuerte
que me asalta dormida
el olor a orégano

I felt myself a queen bee when I woke
I buzzed
capered in the air.
I began to fly high
to descend
to feel myself besieged
by the drones
and I flew higher
I transformed into flame
and fluttered
it was the ancient millenial language
of the enamoured body
the vertigo,
the pain
the piercing joy
I wept with my wounds
felt the sting
of the trap
the impact of the stone
thrown at random
but I also danced
with madness
with the winged specter
of death.
The five senses inflamed me.
The scent of basil was so strong
it assailed me while I slept.
The smell of oregano

a tomillo
pero también
el olor acre
del sudor del macho
fue ese olor a apio
en el que ardí
una noche
en un baile
de cierto barrio prohibido.
¿Y qué decir de los azules
del azul eléctrico turquesa
de aquel témpano
brotando desde el mar?
Era el frío
el abismo
la ballena
el azul me condujo
hacia el abismo
hacia el negro abismal
de la ballena.
El rojo en cambio
el rojo
era la infancia
el vestido con vuelos
que yo amaba,
un mediodía caluroso
en que mi padre y yo
sintiéndonos culpables

of thyme
but also
the pungent smell
of male sweat
it was that celery odor
in which I burnt
one night
at a dance
in a certain forbidden quarter.
And what can I say about blue
the electric turquoise blue
of an iceberg
sprouting from the sea?
It was coldness
the abyss
the whale
blue conducted me
into the abyss
into the abysmal black of the whale.
Red on the contrary
red
was my childhood
the dress with frills
I loved
the hot midday
when my father and I
feeling deliciously guilty

compartimos
la única sandía.
Tacto, olfato,
sabor
oído y ojos
los cinco sentidos
me quemaban
me inflamaban de amor
me disparaban.
Creí alcanzar con ellos
la poesía
pero voló
voló.

shared the only watermelon.
Touch, smell,
taste,
ears and eyes
the five senses
seared me
inflamed me with love
catapulted me.
I thought
I could grasp poetry
with them
but it flew
it flew.

IV · MERLIN

Y seguí transitando por el Río
el Río mi camino
yo anhelando ser puente
de pronto
en algún puerto
vislumbré el cucurucho de la alegría
sobre la cabeza
de un hombre solitario
bailando entre la multitud.
Creí reconocerlo
y me acerqué
él me miró muy hondo
extrajo de la manga su varita
y dibujó en el polvo
un pajarito renco.
"Es como tú"
me dijo
"si aprendes a volar
vas a morir mejor".

Merlín
engendro de íncubo
y mujer
me enseñó a dibujar
una mandala
a hacerle reverencias a la luna
a arrancar de cuajo mis cimientos
volverlos a sembrar
en otra parte

IV · MERLIN

And I kept travelling on the River
the River my road
I wanting to be a bridge
Suddenly
in some port
I glimpsed the wizard's cap of happiness
on the head
of a lone man
dancing amidst the crowd.
I thought I recognized him
and drew near
he gave me a searching look
drew a wand from his sleeve
and sketched a lame bird in the dust.
"She is like you,"
he said
"if you learn to fly
you will have a better death."

Merlin
spawn of incubus
and woman
showed me how to draw
a mandala
how to bow to the moon
how to uproot myself
plant my foundations
elsewhere

y siempre estar en casa
pero también me habló de la palabra
de la que vela
y que desvela
de su magia
su ritmo
su sonido
de cómo hay que arrullarla
golpearla
reventarla.

Un torbellino oscuro
es el lenguaje
forma y magia
lo mismo
un torbellino a veces luminoso
pletórico de orígenes
fulgores
y música
y presagios
un torbellino
queriendo abrirse paso
y arrastrar a los otros
y asomarse al abismo
y asaltar las estrellas.
El burrito se expresa
con un rebuzno tosco
que nos hace reír
cuando acaso habría que llorar.

and always be at home
but he also spoke to me of the word
the word that covers
and discovers
of its magic
its rhythm
its sound
of how you have to cradle it
hammer it
smash it.

A dark whirlwind
language
form and magic
the same
a whirlwind sometimes luminous
plethoric with origins
splendour
and music
and omens
a whirlwind
trying to open a path
and drag others with it
and peer into the abyss
and assail the stars.
The donkey expresses himself
with a crude braying
that makes us laugh
when perhaps we should cry.

El pájaro en cambio
nos incita
a recordar nuestro futuro
nos recoge su canto
nos recoge su vuelo
sus notas recortadas
nos proponen
convertir las palabras
en destellos.

Era hechicero el viejo
era implacable
me iba despojando
de todos mis ropajes
me envolvía en palabras
me lanzaba en pos de la poesía
descendí hasta el abismo
me invadieron imágenes
insólitas:
Teotl
que hizo brotar el fuego
Lilith
y Kukulkán
los pájaros dulces que lloraban
cuando moría una niña.

Volví a la superficie
me sumergí de nuevo:
calaveras

The bird instead
incites us
to recall our future
we withdraw with its song
we withdraw with its flight
its clearcut notes
propose
we polish words
into flashes.

The old man was a wizard
was implacable
he stripped me of my heavy garb
enwrapped me in words
and launched me on the search for poetry
I dove into the abyss
strange images invaded me:
Teotl
who created fire
Lilith
and Kukulkán
the sweet birds who wept
when a baby girl died.

I rose to the surface
and dove down once more:
skulls

pirámides
tierra seca
agrietada.
Me disfracé de bruja
de jaguar
de serpiente
y seguía buceando
y encontré mi nágual
pero a nadie le digo el nombre de mi nágual
a nadie jamás se lo diré.

pyramids
fissured wasteland.
I disguised myself as witch
jaguar
serpent
and kept on diving
and I found my *nagual*
but I told nobody the name of my *nagual*
and I will never tell it to anyone.

V · LA TORRE

Volví a salir a flote
y me esperabas Tú.
Fuiste el imán
mordido por la luna
la herradura golpeándome
en el vientre
una ampolla hormigueante
un llamado a la sangre
de alzar velas
y vuelos.
Merlín lo adivinó
frías estrellas
brotaron de sus ojos
agujetas de hielo
de sus labios.
Extrajo de la manga
su varita
y de un golpe seco
me enclaustró
en una torre inexpugnable.
Se volvió Fafner con escamas
custodiando su presa.
Día y noche
acechando el espacio
envenenando el aire
con eructos de fuego.
Forró de espejos
los muros de la torre

V · THE TOWER

I came to the surface again
and You awaited me.
You were the magnet
bitten out by the moon
The horseshoe hitting me
in the womb
an itching blister
a call of the blood
to hoist sails
and cast off.
Merlin divined it
icy stars
shot from his eyes
icicles
from his lips.
He pulled his wand
from a sleeve
and with a single gesture
encloistered me
in an impregnable tower.
He transformed into scaly Fafnir
guarding his prey.
Day and night
keeping watch
poisoning the air
with fiery belching.
He lined
the tower's walls
with mirrors

me quería inalcanzable
enyomismada me quería
pero había sido quemada
por el Amor
y él sólo cristales me ofrecía
vidrios rotos
palabras
y mandalas
y lunas.

Envuelta en mi silencio
vi mi rostro mil veces repetido
me aburrí de mi rostro
y rompí los espejos.
Uno a uno
los fui rompiendo todos
quería verte a ti
a ti que me rondabas
llamándome
citándome.
Una sola ventana
en lo alto de la torre
ni un hueco
ni una grieta
ni una piedra móvil
miraba mis fragmentos
en los espejos rotos
nunca el rostro completo

he wanted me unreachable
wanted me to preen myself
but I had been burnt
by Love
and he only offered me shards:
bits of glass
words
and mandalas
and moons.

Enwrapped in my silence
I saw my face repeated
a thousand times
I grew bored with my face
and shattered the mirrors.
One by one
I broke them all
I wanted to see you
you who were circling about me
calling out to me
summoning me.
A single window
at the top of the tower
not another hole
nor crack
nor so much as a loose stone
I gazed at my fragments
in the shattered mirrors
never the complete face

solamente fragmentos:
un ojo encapotado
un pedazo de labio
donde ardía tu beso.
Aún estaba tibio
el roce de tus dedos
en mi piel
aún podía oler
el ondeante humo
que anduvo viajando
en tus pulmones.
Lloré
grité
salté
fui una gata en celo
frotándome en los muros
una gata rabiosa
inventando cabriolas
escalé las paredes
con mis uñas
se empinaban los árboles
a verme
me asomé a la ventana
y no te vi
solo Fafner amortajado en su rencor.
Recordé tus palabras
manojos de claveles
tus palabras
golpeándome los párpados.

only fragments:
a clouded eye
a bit of lip
burning with your kiss.
The brush of your fingers
was still warm
on my skin
I could still scent
the wisps of smoke
that travelled
through your lungs.
I wept
screamed
pounced
I was a cat in heat
rubbing against the walls
a raging cat
inventing capers
I scaled the walls
with my claws
the trees lifted their crowns
to watch me
I peered out the window
and didn't see you
only Fafnir shrouded with rancour.
I recalled your words
bunches of carnations
your words
beating against my eyelids.

It's now
or never
me dijiste
Tus palabras
martillando mis oídos:
Now or never
¡Now!

La noche estaba oscura
y me arrojé al vacío
con la boca salada
de terror
pero volé
volé.

"It's now
or never,"
you told me.
Your words
hammering in my ears:
"Now or never,
"Now!"

The night was pitch dark
and I flung myself into emptiness
my mouth salty
with terror
but I flew
I flew.

VI · VASIJA Y FUENTE

De pronto río abajo
acompañada
¿era el Nilo
el Mississippi
el Orinoco?
Todos los ríos
mi Río
y yo vasija henchida
vasijera
barco que no hace ruido
no se agita
va esculpiendo un destino
en su interior.
Silencio
oscuridad
preguntas sueltas:
¿cómo será su pelo
sus manitas?
Asombrada me siento
ante el milagro
ante el vientre que crece
y le da forma
y todo sin esfuerzo
quedamente
mi vasija creciendo
ya soy nido
donadora de vida
cáliz
puente

VI · CHALICE AND FOUNT

Suddenly downstream
this time accompanied
Was it the Nile
the Mississippi
the Orinoco?
All rivers
my River
and I a swelling chalice
a potter
a noiseless vessel
gliding softly
sculpting another destiny.
Silence
darkness
fragmentary questions:
what color the hair?
how the hands?
I am astonished
at the miracle
at the swelling womb
creating form
effortlessly
quietly
my vessel growing
I am a nest
a giver of life
chalice
bridge

¿será hombre
mujer?
¿Tendrá la piel morena
el cabello cobrizo?
Saboreo el momento
voy creando futuro
encadeno el pasado
y el presente
es un codo del Río insospechado
me gusta el mundo
visto desde allí
desde ese puerto espejo.
Amo a los hombres
a las bestias
a las aves
converso por las noches
con la luna
yo misma soy la luna
luna llena
inviolable
donadora de vida
vasijera.

Me recibí de madre
con dolor
empezaron mis pechos
a crecer
eran fuentes mis pechos
se henchían

will it be a boy
a girl?
Will the skin be brown
the hair copper-colored?
I savor the moment
I am creating future
enchaining past
and present
an unexpected curve of the river
I love the world
seen from such angle
from that mirror haven
I love all mankind
and the beasts
and the birds
at night I converse
with the moon
I myself the moon
the full moon
inviolable
donor of life
potter.

I enter motherhood
with pain
my breasts began to swell:
fountains my breasts
distending

se vaciaban
mi hija los vaciaba
mientras yo la acunaba
y me acunaba a mí la Madre Grande
no hay espacio
no hay tiempo
sencillamente somos
me concentro en su oreja
en las circondulaciones
de su oreja
¿cómo es posible?
me pregunto
¿cómo fui capaz
de modelar la perfección?
Me siento diosa omnipotente
sólo mi hija
y yo
me necesita ella
la necesito yo
somos parte de un plan
que no comprendo
ni necesito comprender.

emptying
my daughter emptied them
while I cradled her
and the Great Mother cradled me
there is no space
nor time
we simply are
I concentrate on her ear
on the circumvolutions
of her ear.
How is it possible?
I ask myself
How was I able
to model perfection?
I feel myself omnipotent goddess
only my daughter
and me
she needs me
I need her
we are part of a plan
I cannot comprehend
nor do I need to.

VII · LA COYOTA

Navego por el tiempo
no es el Río
es el tiempo
es la tierra baldía
que me secó los pechos
que marchitó mi vientre
que doblegó mi cuerpo.
Voy husmeando
trotando
todo lo abandoné
me abandonaron
de lejos el llanto de mi hija
no soy madre
ni hija
soy coyota
ni un cactus
ni un arroyo
sólo deseos reprimidos
sueños que yo misma
asesiné.

Debo encerrar con llave
mis recuerdos
La soledad adversa
me acompaña
pude quedarme con los míos
aceptar la derrota
saberme desahuciada

VII · THE COYOTE

I am navigating through time
not the River
but time
it is the waste-land
the desert
which dried my breasts
withered my womb
bent my body.
I sniff
as I trot along
I abandoned everything
I was abandoned
in the distance my daughter's cry
I am neither mother
nor daughter
I am a coyote
not a single cactus
nor a rivulet in sight
only repressed desires
dreams I myself
assassinated.

I must lock up
my memories.
Adverse solitude
surrounds me
I might have stayed with my people
accepted defeat
hopelessness

me duelen las heridas
me revuelco en el polvo
un viento seco azota.
A lo lejos
muy lejos
el llanto de mi hija:
"Duérmete mi niña
cabeza de ayote
que si no te duermes
te come el coyote."

Sigo trotando
buscando
rastreando los huesos
de Vallejo
ras
ras
ras
rastreando.
Don Alex Sinegú
que leía las manos
me auguró esta sequía.

Un abismo a mi lado
al fondo

my wounds are painful
I roll in the dust
a dry wind lashes me.
In the distance
the far distance
the weeping of my daughter:
"*Duérmete mi niña*
cabeza de ayote
que si no te duermes
te come el coyote."
"Go to sleep my baby
my little pumpkin head
if you don't go to sleep
the coyote will eat you."

I keep on trotting
searching
tracking down the bones
of Vallejo
trak
trak
trak
tracking
don Alex Sinegú
who read palms
predicted this drought.

An abyss beside me
in the depths

vidrios rotos
doy una vuelta
al borde del abismo
me asomo
me retraigo
mi imagen no se expande
se la chupa el espejo
los fragmentos trizados
del espejo.
Huyo despavorida
de pronto un cactus florecido
quedamente me acerco
una florcita roja
recuerdo el hibisco
en el patio de mi casa
pero este gozo
es mío
sólo mío
no puedo compartirlo.
La nostalgia me asalta
yo le ladro
me enredo en las raíces
recuerdo a la vieja pordiosera
que me ofreció una rosa
y sigo hacia adelante
husmeando
trotando
rastreando

shards of broken glass
I turn about
at the edge of the abyss
I peer down
I withdraw
my image doesn't expand
the mirror swallows it
shattered fragments
of the mirror.
I flee terrified.
Suddenly a flowering cactus
I approach cautiously
a red flower
I remember the hibiscus
in the patio of my home
but this joy
is mine
mine alone
I can't share it.
Nostalgia pounces
I bark at it
entangle myself in roots
remember the old beggar lady
who offered me a rose
and I keep going
sniffing
trotting
tracking

pasa corriendo un conejo
¿tendré el mismo valor
para el próximo salto?

Un huesito por fin
y otro
y otro
huesos desparramados
por el polvo
los empujo
los junto
con paciencia los junto
un montón de huesos
frente a mí
huesos blancos
y secos
que han perdido su aroma
un túmulo de huesos
a los que yo les canto
el aire del desierto
se esponja con mi canto
y lo devuelve en ecos.
Continúo cantando
conjurando
hasta que siento la mirada
de la luna
y levanto el hocico
y le aúllo a la luna.

a rabbit runs past me
will I have the same courage
for the next leap?

A bone at last
and another
and another
bones scattered
in the dust
I push them
gather them together
patiently gather them
a heap of bones
before me
dry white bones
that have lost their aroma
a mound of bones I sing to
the desert air
sponges up my song
and returns it in echos.
I keep on singing
conjuring
until I sense the gaze
of the moon
and I lift my muzzle
and howl at the moon.

VIII · OJO DE CUERVO

Soy el ojo del cuervo
el persistente ojo
recorriendo
fugitivos instantes
de mi tiempo.
Domino con mis alas
el espacio
a mi tiempo domino
al que me fue otorgado
a esa breve cuerda
que se tensa
entre nacer
y morir.
El pasado es mi tiempo
soy la flecha
me dispara el pasado
debo recuperarlo
recorrer mis recuerdos
con los ojos:
El Izalco a lo lejos
humo hirviente saliendo del volcán
eructando el volcán
llameando
eructando
arrojando piedras
de sus fauces
piedras anaranjadas
rodando por sus flancos
brincando

VIII · THE CROW'S EYE

I am the crow's eye
the persistent eye
scanning
fugitive instants of my time.
I dominate space
with my wings
dominate the time
granted me
the brief bowstring
tensing
between birth
and death.
The past is my time
I am the arrow
triggered by the past
I must recover it
run through memories
with my eyes:
Izalco in the distance
smoke boiling up from the crater
the volcano belching
flaming
belching
spewing boulders
from its maw
orange-red rocks
rolling down its flanks
leaping

tronando cuesta abajo
mientras llora cenizas el volcán
y yo evitando el humo
me desvío a la plaza.

Una lluvia fina
de cenizas
cotonas blancas
hacinadas en la plaza
son los hombres de Izalco
son los niños
limpiándose su rostro
con pañuelos
traca-traca-trac
la tartamuda
van cayendo cotonas
decenas
centenares de cotonas
que caen
se retuercen
inmóviles se quedan.
Aún hay algunas
caminando
rodeando los cadáveres
esperando su turno
caminando en puntillas
para no atropellar
a los cadáveres.

thundering down the slope
while the volcano weeps ashes
and I avoiding the smoke
detour to the plaza.

A fine rain
of ashes
white cotton tunics
crammed into the plaza
they are the men of Izalco
and their sons
wiping their faces
with kerchiefs
traca-traca-trac
the stammerer
the tunics crumple
dozens
hundreds of tunics
falling
writhing
remaining immobile.
Some are still walking
avoiding the cadavers
waiting their turn
walking on tiptoe
to avoid stumbling
against the dead.

Un niño con su padre
de la mano los dos
un niño que no entiende
y mira con ojos desorbitados.

Levanto el vuelo
y me alejo
me alejo.

Llega hasta mí el sollozo del poeta
su voz inconfundible:
España, aparta de mí este cáliz
y estoy en Guernica
en Bilbao
en Madrid
vuelo por las ruinas de Guernica
madres dando alaridos
cadáveres de niños
polvo subiendo de las ruinas
polvo como cenizas
chimeneas en Auschwitz
en Belsen
en Buchenwald
arrojando cenizas
humo negro
y cenizas
de judíos que arden
se consumen

A boy hand in hand
with his father
a child who doesn't understand
and gazes wide-eyed.

I beat my wings
and fly away
fly away.

The poet's sob reaches me
his unmistakeable voice:
Spain, take this chalice from my lips
and I am in Guernica
in Bilbao
Madrid
I fly over the ruins of Guernica
mothers shrieking
dust rising from the ruins
dust like ashes
chimneys in Auschwitz
in Belsen
in Buchenwald
vomiting ashes
black smoke
and the ashes
of Jews who burn
and are consumed

años
décadas de cenizas
pegándose a los rostros
a los automóviles pulidos
de los nazis
que se empeñan en vano
en inmolar un pueblo
y como una flor
llevan la calavera
en sus solapas.
¿Por qué me sigue importando
este planeta?

La época del progreso
nació con Hiroshima
con la bomba atómica en Hiroshima
con el hongo anaranjado
que floreció en un milésimo de segundo
y en los escasos muros que aguantaron
dejó grabadas las sombras
de sus víctimas.
Miles de muertos
en Hiroshima
millares de seres vivos
transformados en cenizas
en espirales de cenizas
en llamas que se descargan
sobre el viento

years
decades of ashes
clinging to the faces
to the polished autos
of the Nazis
who seek in vain
to immolate a people
and like a flower
wear the death's head
in their lapels.
Why should I still care
for this planet?

The era of progress
was born in Hiroshima
with the atomic bomb in Hiroshima
with the orange mushroom
flowering in a thousandth
of a second
leaving the shadows of its victims
engraved on the remaining walls.
Thousands of dead
in Hiroshima
thousands
and thousands of living beings
transformed into ashes
into spirals of ash
into flames discharging
in the wind

el reino de la muerte
aquí en la tierra
el zumbido oscuro
de la muerte
un seis de agosto
en la mañana.

Sigo volando a la deriva
la niña de Vietnam
envuelta en llamas
vuelo más alto
espero
judíos persiguiendo palestinos
serbios diezmando musulmanes
cúmulos de cadáveres
bloqueando senderos
en Rwanda
los tambores tribales
su tam-tam
me poso sobre un árbol
ya no hay bosque
algunos árboles ralos
que subsisten
llueve sobre los árboles
es ácida la lluvia
envenena los ríos
envenena los mares
está enferma la tierra
contemplo el horizonte

the kingdom of death
here on earth
the dull droning of death
one sixth of August
in the morning.

I fly aimlessly
the small Vietnamese girl
enwrapped in flames
I fly higher
waiting
Jews persecuting Palestinians
Serbs decimating Muslims
piles of cadavers
blocking the roads
in Rwanda
tribal drums
tam-tamming
I alight on a tree
the forest is gone
a few rachitic trees
survive
an acid rain falls on the trees
poisons rivers
poisons the seas
the earth is ill
I scan the horizon

rayitos fugitivos
de esperanza
de amor
de valentía
rayitos contagiosos
que a pesar de la lluvia
no dejan de brillar:
revolución de claveles
en Lisboa
de estudiantes en Cuba
en París
Nicaragua
la figura del chino
y su carpeta
enfrentándose él solo
a los tanques que marchan
en Pequín
los Beatles
sus canciones
John Lennon predicando
"hagamos el amor
y no la guerra".

Emprendo el vuelo de regreso
nada ha cambiado
nada:
escuadrones de muerte
bombardeos
miseria

fugitive rays
of hope
of love
of courage
contagious rays
keep sparkling
despite the rain:
the revolution of carnations
in Lisbon
of students in Cuba
in Paris
Nicaragua
the lone Chinaman
with briefcase
confronting the column of tanks
in Peking
the Beatles
their songs
John Lennon preaching
"make love
not war."

I start the return flight
nothing has changed
nothing:
squadrons of death
bombardments
misery

Tlatelolco
Sumpul
los niños desechables
se me nublan los ojos
se me nubla el paisaje
masacre en El Mozote
en Tenancingo
en Wiwilí
el polvo de tus calles
Tenancingo
en hálito de muerte
se trocó.

Where have all the flowers gone?

Tlatelolco
Sumpul
expendable children.
My eyes cloud over
the landscape clouds
massacres in El Mozote
in Tenancingo
in Wiwilí
the dust of your streets
Tenancingo
into an exhalation of death
has turned.

Where have all the flowers gone?

IX · LA MARIPOSA

Ya la ceiba no existe
derrumbaron mi ceiba
se hicieron añicos los espejos
eché a secar mi Río
y se escondió la luna.
Estoy vacía de deseos
mi espada
en su estuche de satén.
¿Por qué ahora
por qué
busca seducirme
la poesía?
Entró por la ventana
y se posó en mi mano
la miré con nostalgia
se entreabrieron mis labios
y con un leve soplo
la alejé.

IX · THE BUTTERFLY

The Ceiba no longer exists
they cut down my Ceiba
the Mirrors shattered
I dried my River
and the Moon hid itself.
I am empty of desires
my sword rests
in its satin case.
Why now?
why
does poetry come to taunt me?
She entered by the window
poised in my hand
I gazed at her with nostalgia
pursed my lips
and with a breath
sent her on her way.

Curbstone Press, Inc.

is a non-profit publishing house dedicated to literature that reflects a commitment to social change, with an emphasis on contemporary writing from Latin America and Latino communities in the United States. Curbstone presents writers who give voice to the unheard in a language that goes beyond denunciation to celebrate, honor and teach. Curbstone builds bridges between its writers and the public – from inner-city to rural areas, colleges to community centers, children to adults. Curbstone seeks out the highest aesthetic expression of the dedication to human rights and intercultural understanding: poetry, testimonials, novels, stories, photography.

This mission requires more than just producing books. It requires ensuring that as many people as possible know about these books and read them. To achieve this, a large portion of Curbstone's schedule is dedicated to arranging tours and programs for its authors, working with public school and university teachers to enrich curricula, reaching out to underserved audiences by donating books and conducting readings and community programs, and promoting discussion in the media. It is only through these combined efforts that literature can truly make a difference.

Curbstone Press, like all non-profit presses, depends on the support of individuals, foundations, and government agencies to bring you, the reader, works of literary merit and social significance which might not find a place in profit-driven publishing channels. Our sincere thanks to the many individuals who support this endeavor and to the following organizations, foundations and government agencies: ADCO Foundation, Witter Bynner Foundation for Poetry, Connecticut Commission on the Arts, Connecticut Arts Endowment Fund, Ford Foundation, Greater Hartford Arts Council, Junior League of Hartford, Lawson Valentine Foundation, LEF Foundation, Lila Wallace-Reader's Digest Fund, The Andrew W. Mellon Foundation, National Endowment for the Arts, Puffin Foundation, and United Way-Windham Region.

Please support Curbstone's efforts to present the diverse voices and views that make our culture richer. Tax-deductible donations can be made to Curbstone Press, 321 Jackson St., Willimantic, CT 06226. Telephone: (860) 423-5110.